Author, playwright, translator, theater and film director Roger Pulvers received his MA in Russian Studies at Harvard Graduate School and did post-graduate work at Warsaw University in Poland before arriving in Japan in the summer of 1967. He has published more than fifty books in Japanese and English, including novels such as *The Death of Urashima Taro*, *General Yamashita's Treasure*, *Star Sand*, *Liv*, *The Dream of Lafcadio Hearn* and *Peaceful Circumstances*.

In 2017 the feature film of *Star Sand*, written and directed by him, had wide release throughout Japan and screened on primetime Japanese television. He is also the author of two memoirs: *My Japan: a cultural memoir* and *The Unmaking of an American*, both published by Balestier Press.

Roger has worked extensively in radio, film and television. He was assistant to director Oshima Nagisa on the film *Merry Christmas, Mr. Lawrence* and co-wrote the script for *Ashita e no Yuigon* (Best Wishes for Tomorrow), for which he won the Crystal Simorgh Prize for Best Script at the 27th Fajr International Film Festival in Tehran.

Roger received the prestigious Miyazawa Kenji Prize in 2008 and the Noma Award for the Translation of Japanese Literature in 2013; in 2018, Japan's highest honor, the Order of the Rising Sun; and in 2019, the Order of Australia. Over the past fifty years he has translated prose, drama and poetry from Japanese, Russian and Polish, and his plays have been widely performed in Australia, Japan and the United States.

ALSO BY ROGER PULVERS

Liv
Half of Each Other
The Honey and the Fires
The Dream of Lafcadio Hearn
Peaceful Circumstances
The Unmaking of an American
My Japan: a cultural memoir
The Charter—and Thirteen Other Stories about Japan

TRANSLATIONS

Night on the Milky Way Train and Nine Other Stories
The Boy of the Winds and Other Stories
The Illusions of Self: Tanka by Takuboku Ishikawa
Wholly Esenin: Poems by Sergei Esenin
Poems 2020: Translations from Russian, Polish and Japanese

THE GOVERNMENT INSPECTOR
FOR TWO ACTORS

Translated from the original play in Russian
The Government Inspector
by **NIKOLAI GOGOL**
and adapted for two actors by

ROGER PULVERS

BALESTIER PRESS
LONDON · SINGAPORE

Balestier Press
Centurion House, London TW18 4AX
www.balestier.com

The Government Inspector for Two Actors:
Translated from the original play in Russian, The Government Inspector
by Nikolai Gogol, and adapted for two actors
Copyright © Roger Pulvers, 2022

A CIP catalogue record for this book
is available from the British Library.

ISBN 978 1 913891 26 8

Cover illustration by Lucy Pulvers

All rights reserved. No part of this publication may be reproduced, stored in a retrieval system or transmitted in any form or by any means, electronic or mechanical, without the prior written permission of the publisher of this book.

Any reading or production of this play requires the written permission of the translator. Please direct enquires to Balestier Press.

Emoto Akira as the mayor and Hashizume Isao as his wife
Tokyo, Theater X (Cai), 2000

Darren Gilshenan (left) as Bobchinsky and William Zappa as the mayor
Photo by Wendy McDougall
Bell Shakespeare Company, Australian tour, 2007

From the Productions

Jake Speer as Khlestakov and Brandon McClelland as the mayor's daughter (in rehearsal)
Roxy Theatre, Leeton, 2012

Contents

FROM THE PRODUCTIONS

5

FOREWORD

11

INTRODUCTION

17

LIST OF CHARACTERS

21

THE GOVERNMENT INSPECTOR FOR TWO ACTORS

23

FOREWORD

I first translated Nikolai Gogol's *The Government Inspector* back in 1981 while working as Playwright-in-Residence and a director at The Playbox Theatre in Melbourne. I had loved this play since reading it as a graduate student while at Harvard's Russian Research Center in 1964.

The play is always performed with a large cast covering the many colorful characters, but I knew that we could not afford that luxury. I decided to reduce the number of performers to eight. Having translated the play and managing to make it performable with eight actors, I presented the script to the theater's artistic director, my dear friend then and now, Carrillo Gantner, who had brought me into the Playbox in the late seventies.

"It's great," he said, "but we're now more constrained financially than before. Could you possibly get it down to four actors?"

"Um, I think so," I said, taking the typed script back from him.

But I thought: What if the same thing happens again? Life in the theater is always on a knife edge. This was Giacometti, not Rubens.

I figured that, if it could be adapted—always faithfully to the spirit of the original—for four actors, why not for two, so long as the mise-en-scène is constantly kept in mind. After all, this play is about identity and imposture. Who can say who is who, and why they are where they are and not somewhere else? This has to be the ultimate question relating to individuals and society in our day and age.

Unfortunately, I left The Playbox in June 1982 to be assistant to Oshima Nagisa on his film *Merry Christmas, Mr. Lawrence* and moved back to Japan in November of that year. The typescript of *The Government Inspector for Two Actors* went into my drawer in my home in Tokyo.

I directed a number of plays in Tokyo in the following years, including Strindberg's *Miss Julie* (with the wonderful actor Kishida Kyoko, star of *Woman in the Dunes*, in the lead), Witkiewicz's *In the Little Manor* (again with Kishida Kyoko and also with Hashizume Isao, later to be Khlestakov in my production of Gogol) and Sam Shepard's *Buried Child*. But the chance to direct *The Government Inspector for Two Actors* didn't arise ... not until 2000, when Ueda Misako, artistic director of Theater X (Cai) in Tokyo, asked me to do it. I had translated and directed Strindberg's *Dance of Death* there earlier that year. This was for the Bell Shakespeare Company. We had opened in February of that year at the Adelaide Festival, and, after touring to Tokyo and Nagoya, took the production to Canberra.

The first production of *The Government Inspector for Two Actors* took place at Theater X (Cai) in June 2000, naturally in Japanese. The two actors were Hashizume Isao and Emoto Akira, both extremely well known on stage and screen. The production was filmed and aired on Japan's national broadcaster, NHK.

It may seem strange to people unfamiliar with the history of modern theater in Japan that the Japanese have long loved Western plays and have been performing them to large audiences ever since the late Meiji era (1868-1912). Gogol alone made an enormous impact on Japanese literature and theater. Translations of his works ran into scores of editions. One of author Akutagawa Ryunosuke's most famous short stories is "The Nose," adapted from the Gogol original. Renowned translator Yonekawa Masao, whole popularized the works of Dostoevsky, Pushkin, Tolstoy and Chekhov in Japan, published his Japanese version of *The Government Inspector* in a paperback edition from Iwanami Shoten in 1928. The play has even been performed, as late as December 2021, on the Noh stage.

A few years after the Theater X (Cai) production, John Bell, founder of Bell Shakespeare, phoned me and asked if they could mount a production in 2007. I was, needless to say, thrilled.

"I'll be directing it," said John. "Is that all right?"

"Well ... actually, I've wanted to direct it too, but ..."

"I'd like permission to do it," he said.

I knew John to be a director of genius and felt that the play would be in the best of hands.

The Bell Shakespeare production toured Australia, including a long run at the Sydney Opera House. The actors were William Zappa and Darren Gilshenan. William was a close friend who had acted in several of my plays in Melbourne. He was a brilliant Brecht in my musical *Bertolt Brecht Leaves Los Angeles*. I had seen Darren on stage any number of times. He is a comic actor of amazing resources and depth. I was particularly thrilled when the production played in Canberra, where I had lived for seven years in the 1970s and had begun my career in the theater.

During the first decade of this century I was commuting to Tokyo from Sydney, writing books, translating, doing some radio and television here and there, and working in film in Japan. The only theater I did was a production, in 2004, of two plays that I wrote in Japanese, *Kawaramachi Story* and *The Reporters*. I directed these at Theater X (Cai), and we took the production to the Studio Theatre at the National Institute of Dramatic Art (NIDA), our world-class theater arts school in Sydney, with a tour to Adelaide as well. It was the first time for an Australian—or, I believe, for any nonJapanese—playwright to write plays in Japanese and take them to their own country. I guess that's the story of my life.

Early in 2011 I received an email from Jake Speer. Jake was a student at NIDA. He said that he was writing from Australia and that he wished to put on a production of *The Government Inspector for*

Two Actors in Leeton, a small town in the Riverina region of Australia about five hundred and fifty kilometers by road from Sydney. Jake had been unaware that I was Australian. While I had never been to Leeton, I knew about the town from having bought Letona-brand tinned peaches while living in Canberra in the 1970s.

I was in Tokyo when Jake's email reached me but was about to fly back for a short stay in Sydney and suggested that we meet. Jake came to my home in the suburb of Pymble.

"There is this amazing theater in Leeton called The Roxy. It's kind of gone into disuse and, being from Leeton myself, I want to revive it by putting on a play there, your Gogol. I've got another actor, and there's a great director in Wagga Wagga who will direct."

I watched some video clips of Jake's performances and could see that he was a young actor of immense talent. I gladly gave him the go-ahead. The other actor was Brandon McClelland, Jake's fellow student at NIDA. As it turned out, the director pulled out and I ended up taking his place.

We had our first readings of the play in my study in Pymble, and I could tell from the outset that Jake and Brandon were, with their broad skills and profound instincts, amazingly suited not only to the many supporting parts but also to the parts of the wily and cunning inspector and the equally wily and cunning mayor.

I flew out to Leeton—it's only an hour's flight from Sydney—toward the end of December 2011, moving into the Historic Hydro Hotel, a stunning building constructed in 1919. The town of Leeton was designed by Walter Burley Griffin, the American architect who created the plan for the nation's new capital, Canberra. The water towers that you can see just outside your Hydro window were designed by him as well.

The Government Inspector for Two Actors played in Leeton in January 2012 at the Roxy, an art deco gem that opened its doors on 7 April 1930 with a film (John Ford's *The Black Watch*, starring Myrna Loy and Victor McLaglen). "The Irrigator," the local newspaper, gave us prime publicity. The town mayor was in the audience on opening night; and, after the performance, he came up to me and whispered in my ear, "If I'da known what the mayor's wife was up to when I went away, I'da never left town!"

Jake and Brandon were, in a word, magnificent. We played Wagga Wagga too, but I had to return to Tokyo after the Leeton show, so I didn't see it there. Subsequently, in 2016, I was able to bring Brandon to Japan to play the lead nonJapanese role in my film *Star Sand*.

The Government Inspector for Two Actors is a theatrical challenge to actors and staff, especially costume designer and stage manager. It requires ultra-quick changes. The challenge lies not only in getting the actor into the right costume at the right time, but also for the actors to transform themselves instantaneously from one character to another. But the script was constructed with all this in mind from the beginning. Its premise is that you can be anybody you want to be, so long as you can convince others of it.

In that sense *The Government Inspector for Two Actors* is about the theater itself as much as it is about the true and false faces of our society.

INTRODUCTION
The Government Inspectors in our Midst

Ever since the first performance of Nikolai Gogol's *The Government Inspector* took place on 19 April 1836, Russia and the world have been fascinated by Khlestakov, a character in the play who poses as a government inspector and gets away with murder ... or, if not murder, at least pretty much everything short of it.

The original idea for the play had come to Gogol from Pushkin, who suggested the theme of both *The Government Inspector* and his other classic, the novel *Dead Souls*.

The story is a simple one.

One day Khlestakov, a petty official from the capital, arrives in a provincial Russian town and sets himself up at the hotel. He is presumably on his way to visit his uncle in Saratov. He has no money, having lost everything at cards but the shirt off his back. Just as his credit evaporates and he fears that he will be tossed into jail, a miracle happens: The people of the town—beginning with the corrupt mayor, his charmingly aggressive wife and his sweet romantic young daughter—take Khlestakov for an important bureaucrat, a government inspector. They believe that he is on official business to report the goings-on in their town; and they set out to pull the wool over his eyes with bribes (in the case of the mayor and the townspeople) or (in the case of the wife and daughter) seduce him for their own intense gratification.

The ways in which Khlestakov and the people of the town court, swindle and cajole each other form the theme and drama of this blackest of comedies.

Nikolai Gogol himself was a provincial, born in a Ukrainian village in 1809. As such, his use of the Russian language was often somewhat bizarre, stylistically fresh and fetchingly off center. There is a folksiness about it, but also a wonderful whimsy, the wit of the outsider trapped in the kinds of mindless and deadly games that the powerful and slick of the city—and the unscrupulous and sly of the country—play. He was acknowledged during his short lifetime—he died, age forty-two, in 1852—as a brilliant storyteller; and his novel *Dead Souls*, published in 1842, was an immense popular and critical success. Subsequently, his short stories, particularly "The Nose" and "The Overcoat," deeply influenced many Russian and nonRussian authors. It wouldn't be an exaggeration to say that twentieth-century literature began, in the previous century, with Nikolai Gogol.

Transported to the twentieth century, Gogol would certainly have become a writer like Mikhail Bulgakov or Vladimir Nabokov. (In fact, Gogol had, at one time, considered emigrating to America, as Nabokov did; and Nabokov, for his part, wrote a biography of Gogol.) Or Gogol might have become an Albert Camus, another writer brought up on the outskirts of an empire, in his case Algeria, then a colony of France. Camus, too, wrote about society's "little people."

As we approach *The Government Inspector* from our vantage point in the twenty-first century, we can see its main character, Khlestakov, in a different and new light.

Khlestakov is surely one of Gogol's "little men," a petty official, a nobody if there ever was one, on his way out of the capital. But his trip has already taken two months. Whatever pleasure comes his way, he seizes; whatever misfortune is sent him, he flees. But where is he really heading? Or, if he does actually arrive at Saratov, what will he do then?

These are the questions that we must ask ourselves in presenting this play today. The hero and other characters of *The Government Inspector* are not quaint hapless people trapped in an old Russian folktale. They are our contemporaries in every sense of the word.

Introduction

We can see Khlestakov as a man truly lost, a man totally lacking in principles, a man who is happy to change his identity to suit any occasion: in other words, the perfect symbol of our day and age. We are surrounded by Khlestakovs in our government, our work places, our schools, our hospitals, our churches. Gogol created not only a type, but an archetype; not only for Russia but for all countries; not only for his era, but for all eras.

Khlestakov's name is taken from the Russian verb *khlestat'*, which has a number of meanings, including "to whip," "to flow along" and "to quaff or swill," all of them admirably applicable to the character.

Perhaps Khlestakov is on his way to nowhere and this is a play not only about the abuses of power but also about the futility of contending with our most rooted of traits: self-aggrandizement for its own sake.

After the opening of *The Government Inspector*, the press and the powers-that-be attacked Gogol, sending him out of the country to Italy, where he remained, for the most part, for some six years. He gave himself over to ascetic and all-consuming religious practices, in the end burning the manuscript of the second volume of *Dead Souls* and, in 1852, on the verge of madness, starving himself to death.

It is through Gogol's own fate as an exile, as well as the fate of the "little people" in his country, that we come to know our very own inspectors of today, the people who choose to live their lives as an arrogant pretense regardless of the cost to others.

Roger Pulvers
Sydney 2022

LIST OF CHARACTERS

[in order of first appearance as A or Z]

Petrov bureaucrat Z

Mayor Anton Antonovich A

Pyotr Ivanovich Bobchinsky postmaster A

Pyotr Ivanovich Dobchinsky Bobchinsky's friend A

Márya Antonovna mayor's daughter Z

Anna Andreyevna mayor's wife Z

Osip Khlestakov's servant A

Ivan Alexandrovich Khlestakov petty public servant Z

Waiter A

Lapkin-Flapkin doctor A

Luka Lukich Khlopov judge A

Teacher A

Chang clothier A

Baker A

Sergeant's wife A

Officer Z

THE GOVERNMENT INSPECTOR FOR TWO ACTORS

In the beginning there is an office. Z, as Petrov, a bureaucrat, is writing in a large notebook. The single naked light bulb in the room suddenly flickers. It stops flickering, and Petrov continues to write. Again it flickers. He is about to get up, when it stops. He writes. The bulb flickers. Petrov stands on a chair to fix the bulb. He can barely reach it. As he tries to fix the bulb, A, as the mayor, silently enters from the back. He approaches Z, who is unaware of his presence. When A speaks to Z, Z gets a fright and hangs onto the light bulb cord. This fixes the bulb.

A Petrov, I have come to inform you of news of a very unpleasant nature. A government inspector is coming to town.

Z What do you mean "government inspector"?

A An inspector. From the government. From St. Petersburg. Incognito. And not only that. He has secret orders to boot.

Z We're in for it now.

A We're in for it now.

Z Oh God. One minute it's quiet as the grave here and suddenly ...

A ... someone comes ...

Z ... and with secret orders to boot.

Z reaches for the revolver in his pocket, but A stops him.

A I somehow suspected that something like this would happen. Last night I dreamt all night long of two enormous rats, two unnatural giants, black all over. They crawled over me, smelled me from head to toe then ... they vanished into thin air. Now I'll read you the letter I received from Chmykov, you know him. "My dear old friend and benefactor ... [*mumbling*] ... to inform you that an official has arrived with instructions to inspect your region. This official will be posing as a private personage. Now, we have all been guilty of little sins of commission, after all, you, as mayor, do not balk at things which slide across your palm. ... (*This line to Petrov.*) Yes, well, I'm not alone in that ... so I advise you to seize every precaution, albeit he may appear at any moment, if, that is, he is not already amongst you incognito! My sister Anna Kirilovna and her husband are staying with us. Ivan Kirilovich has put on a lot of weight and never stops playing the fiddle ..." And so on and so forth. That's the way things stand.

Z again reaches for the revolver, but again A stops him.

Z Very strange situation, very strange. There's more to this than meets the eye. Why should it happen here? Why would a government inspector come here, of all places?

A Why? It's fate, that's why. Until now he's gone somewhere else. Now it's our turn.

Z He's seeking out traitors.

A Traitors? In a place like this? You could travel for three weeks from here without hitting a border, and still be safe inside Mother Russia.

Z No, I'm telling you, they see all.

A But this is my town. I have brought order to this town, with the police and what-have-you. I advise you to take the appropriate steps. The inspector will want to see all the institutions under your supervision.

Z Under my supervision?

A Yes. Courts. Schools. Hospitals. Everything must be clean.

Z I'll launder the patients' nightcaps. It will make them look healthy.

A And put signs up in Latin over each bed, to make it look like we are treating their diseases, when they came down with them, day, date, and what-have-you. And get rid of the really sick ones. I want everybody in the hospital to be healthy.

Z I will take all tolerable measures. "Nature's way is the best way." The human organism is a simple beast. If it gets better, it gets better. If it dies ... it dies.

A What about the courthouse, though? The geese there keep biting the guilty ... I mean, the accused.

Z I'll have them slaughtered.

A The accused?

Z No. The geese.

A And that clerk you have there. Of course he's a very clever man, but he stinks of vodka day and night.

Z He says it's his natural smell. His wet nurse dropped him when he was a baby and he's smelt of vodka ever since.

A What should we do about this letter from Chmykov? What sins was he talking about?

Z I'll make a clean breast of it. I take bribes. But what bribes, I ask you? Borzoi puppies? Is that a sin?

A A puppy is a bribe by any other name.

Z But not, Mayor, like a fur coat worth a barrelful of rubles that a public official receives for his wife....

A What of it? One man takes a bribe in dogs, another in ... some other animal. What about the schools under you, eh? When we teach children about Alexander the Great, all we need to tell them is that he was great.

Z That's the trouble with teachers. They want to have a say in what they teach.

A They've got the strangest ways, if you ask me. There's the one—can't remember his name—with the big fat mug who can't help making weird faces all the time. Now, making weird faces at the pupils is one thing, maybe it's part of their education, who am I to say? But what if he makes these faces at the inspector, eh? There's no telling what the consequences might be. All of this wouldn't matter if that damned incognito wasn't turning up in our midst. He's bound to ask who's in charge of everything. Listen, here's what we must do: Tear down that old fence next to the cobbler's and stick up a police notice to make it look like something is under construction. Oh God, I forgot. Next to that fence there's a huge pile of rubbish. What a stinking awful town this place is! You put up a monument to something or a fence and before you know it the whole place is choking in garbage. And if the visiting official asks your men if they're happy with their work, they are to answer, "Totally happy, Your Honor." And if they don't, I'll give them something to be totally unhappy about later. Oi oi oi, it's one sin after another. Please God, get us through this quickly, and I'll put the biggest candle on the altar you've ever seen. And every damn tradesman in this town will donate three pounds of wax for that candle. And if our visitor asks why there's no chapel in the hospital even though we got the money to build it five years ago, don't forget: we started to build it, but it burnt down. And stop letting the soldiers run around on the streets with just their shirts on and nothing below the waist.

He exits.

Z We're in for it.

Z returns to his desk, puts the revolver on it and sits. He looks through his notebook and rips a page or two out of it. A, as Bobchinsky, the postmaster, enters. A speaks quickly.

A Will somebody please tell me about this inspector who's supposed to be here? I've just been at my post office and heard about it.

Z Is he here already?

A It means war.

Z That's what I said. There's a war starting.

A It's the Turks. We'll crush them.

Z Not the Turks, you blooming idiot. The war's here. It's us who's going to get crushed, not the bloody Turks. It's the mayor they're after. He's the one going around bullying everybody. I've never cheated a soul. Yet someone is informing on me.

A Someone...?

Z approaches A, who backs off.

Z Yes. Why else would an inspector come all the way out here? Listen, Bobchinsky. You're the postmaster.

A I am?

Z Yes.

A Oh, yes!

Z Why couldn't you just unstick some of the letters that pass in and out, for our common benefit. If there's nothing denunciatory about me in them, you could restick them back together again and write "repaired by the post office" or something on them.

A I've been doing that for years, but not as a precautionary measure or anything, just because I like keeping up with people's lives, you know, who's died, who's in ... in ... with who. It makes fascinating reading, you know. Very touching. Much better than reading the newspaper.

Z And you've seen nothing about an inspector coming from St. Petersburg?

A St. Petersburg? Not particularly. But I have a juicy letter from a lieutenant to his mistress about all sorts of things. [*He produces the letter.*] Want to read it?

He is absorbed in reading the letter.

Z Not now, you idiot. But, listen Bobchinsky, if you happen to intercept anything mentioning me, don't let it slip through your fingers, to the mayor, I mean. Pass it on to me.

A is at the door. He opens it.

A Nothing would make me happier.

A exits. Z is now more terrified than ever. He puts the revolver into his mouth ... and is about to pull the trigger when A, as Dobchinsky, enters. A speaks very slowly.

A Something unbelievable has happened. Right out of the blue.

Z Yes, I know.

A Most unforeseeable, I ... you know?

Z Yes. But you tell me, Dobchinsky.

A Well, Bobchinsky and I were entering the hotel. We were entering the hotel ... and, I'll tell you all about it. First, before we entered the hotel, I was strolling along, minding my own business, and I stopped off at Korobkin's place, but as Korobkin wasn't at home,

I went around to Rastakovsky's, but as Rastakovsky wasn't at home, I ...

Z What happened, for Christ's sake? Did he come?

A I'm trying to tell you. So, then I decided to go to the post office to see Pyotr Ivanovich Bobchinsky, but, what do you know, if I didn't see him at the stall where they sell meat pirozhki instead.

Z Meat pirozhki.

A Oh, they have cabbage pirozhki too. The cabbage in them is really ...

Z Dammit, tell me what you saw!

A I'm trying to, but you keep interrupting me. So, I saw Pyotr Ivanovich Bobchinsky by the stall where they sell meat pirozhki ... and cabbage pirozhki. And he says, "Have you heard the news?" and I say, I say, "No, what news?" and he says, he says, "Well, apparently the mayor received a certain letter."

Z I know about the damn letter. What happened next?

A Next? I'm trying to tell you. So, we went into the hotel because Pyotr Ivanovich Bobchinsky's belly was empty and he wanted to eat a salmon.

Z You sure it was salmon?

A [*Pause*] Yeah. And, as we were strolling into the hotel, who did we meet there but a man who was unseemingly elegant, but not in uniform.

The Government Inspector for Two Actors

Z Not in uniform?

A Yes. Not in uniform. So I call over the hotel manager, Vlas, his wife had a baby just three weeks ago, you know, a frisky little boy, he'll manage the hotel just like his dad one day ... and I ask him, "Vlas," I say discreetly, I say, "who is that man not in uniform?" And Vlas answers, "Well, his name is Ivan Alexandrovich Khlestakov, and he's some sort of official from St. Petersburg on his way to see his people in Saratov. He charges everything to his account and he doesn't take his eyes off anybody in our town." And no sooner did Vlas tell me that than it hit me on the head, and I say to Pyotr Ivanovich Bobchinsky, I say, I say, "Aha."

Z What do you mean, "Aha"?

A Well, to tell you the truth, to be absolutely fair, it wasn't me who said that to Pyotr Ivanovich Bobchinsky, it was ...

Z All right.

A No, actually, we both said, "Aha. What is an official from the government doing here when he should be on his way to Saratov?"

Z Who? What official?

A The official. The one in the letter. The government inspector.

Z Oh God. It can't be him.

A It must be. He doesn't pay his bills and he doesn't move on to Saratov. He observes everything. He saw us eating salmon, mainly because of Pyotr Ivanovich's stomach, and he just stood there peering into our plates. Scared the living daylights outta me, I can tell you that.

Z   Lord, forgive us for our sins. What room is he in?

A   Room five, below the stairs.

Z   Same room those visiting policemen had the fight in last year. How long's he been here, you say?

A   Two weeks.

Z   Two weeks, already? Oh God. Since then we've been starving our prisoners. The wife of the sergeant has been beaten up. The streets are filthy. The whole town's a cesspit.

A   Look, why don't you just go down to the hotel now and meet him? [*A is at the door.*] Make a clean breast of it.

A exits.

Z   Why should I? The mayor is the one who should make a clean breast of it. Why should I?

Z sits again. He rips another strip of paper from his notebook, puts it into his mouth and chews it. He picks up the revolver and exits. After a pause, a gunshot is heard.

Scene change—mayor's house

A, as the Mayor, runs in. He speaks to Márya, his daughter, who is offstage.

A Márya, get my coat for me, Márya, and my new hat, and my sword. I must go out to meet an official who is staying at the hotel.

Z enters as Márya. She carries her father's coat and hat, and puts them on him.

Z I'm here, Papa. Oh, Papa. Tell me, what is he like?

A Who?

Z The inspector from St. Petersburg. Does he have a moustache? What kind of moustache, a tickly one or a silky, soft one.

A How should I know. I'll tell you later.

Z Later? I want to know now. Is he a colonel? Is he?

A Go tell your mother to get ready for our guest. Tell her I want nothing spared.

Z You find out, Papa. You find out for me!

Z exits.

A My God, a bunch of no-good phonies in this town. I bet they're cooking up something behind my back right now. Look at this sword, all chipped and scratched. Is that a fit sword for a mayor? It never occurs to anyone to buy me a new one. Why do the women abandon me just when I need help?

A exits. Z enters, as Anna, the mayor's wife, dressed to kill.

Z Have you seen this inspector who is at the hotel? Is he handsome? What color eyes does he have? Does he have a moustache? Anton. Antosha! Where are you? Is he a colonel? [*She leans out the window and calls to her servant.*] Oi, Avdotya, you heard anything about someone arriving here? You haven't? What a fool that girl is! What, he dismissed you with a wave of his hand? What's a wave, you still could've jumped in front of him, couldn't you? What, there are two men in the room? Well, just go and find out, do you hear? Look through the keyhole, find out what color his eyes are, and get straight back here, you hear? Quick, hurry … hurry … hurry!

Scene change—room five at the hotel.

There is a bed. On the bed, under a blanket, is A, as Osip, Khlestakov's servant.

A Ooo, my belly is sounding off like a regimental band of horns and bugles. When are we going to get home again? It's two months since we last saw Petersburg, and all our money's gone down the drain. So we sit in this lousy hotel, and I have to order all the most expensive food for him: "Hey, Osip, run out and order me the best meal in town. Only the best will do me." As if he was really more than a trumped-up little clerk. The first person he meets, out come the cards, and he loses the shirt off our backs. I've had enough of this rat's life. Take me back to Petersburg. Music halls, dancing dogs, whatever your heart desires. In the capital everyone talks so polite and delicate-like, if you've got money. And the women: aaah! Take your pick! But with his lordship, you can't tell if you're coming or going. One day you're eating like a king and the next you're on the verge of starvation, just like right now. And it's all his fault. What can you do with a man like him? He gets some money sent by his uncle, and before you know it, whoosh, he's riding about in cabs, prancing about at the theater every night, and a week later he's flogging his new coat at the flea market. A coat worth a hundred and fifty and he gets a measly twenty for it. And not even a pittance for his trousers. All just so's to avoid working. He'd rather die than set foot in his office. And the card games! And now the hotel manager says he won't give us another crumb till we pay our bill. God, I could swallow the whole world, I'm so hungry. Oh, someone's here. Must be him. [*He jumps off the bed.*]

Z as Khlestakov strolls into the room, taking off his gloves.

Z Here, take these, will you, Osip. And stop sprawling all over my bed.

A Sprawling? I wasn't sprawling. I was lying.

Z Liar. Look, it's all crumpled.

A So what? You think I don't know a bed when I see one? What's your bed to me anyway?

Z Have a look in my pouch. Any tobacco left?

A How could there be? You smoked the last of it four days ago.

Z Listen. Hey, Osip.

A What is it?

Z Be a good servant and go you-know-where.

A Where?

Z Downstairs, dammit. To the kitchen. Tell them to bring me up some dinner.

A Don't feel like going nowhere.

Z What? [*He rushes toward him to strike him.*] You stupid idiot.

A All right, I'll go. But nothing will come of it. The manager said, "No more free meals."

Z How dare he not serve me. Ridiculous.

A The manager said he'll go to the mayor. "Your boss is a phony," he informed me, "a cheater, a parasite."

Z It really makes you happy telling me this, doesn't it. Nincompoop.

A He says he'll go to the police. He says, "Your boss moves into my hotel, lives it up, runs up a bill and then refuses to leave." He says, "I'll see that he doesn't leave ... jail."

Z Simpleton. [*A nods.*] Not him, you. Now get down there and tell him to feed us.

A I'll ask him to come up here to see you.

Z Up here? What for? All right. Bring him up here. [*A exits.*] What a rotten little hole this town is. Everybody I've met is rotten to the core. And there seem to be no women at all except old hags with the body of a cart horse.

There is a knock on the door and A, as waiter, enters.

A The manager has sent me.

Z Good day, my dear chap. Keeping fit?

A Thank you, Sir.

Z And how's the hotel trade? Lots of guests?

A Enough.

Z Listen here, dear boy. They seem to have forgotten about my dinner, just go down and fetch it for me, will you. I've something or other to attend to after dinner, so I must have it immediately.

A The manager said no more meals ... Sir. It appears as though he is going to complain to the mayor about you.

Z Complain? Look, judge for yourself, dear boy. I have got to eat. I will waste away here if I don't eat. Now, go down and persuade the manager.

A How?

Z Tell him that money is no object. It's all right for him. He's just an ordinary peasant. He can go a day without eating. Well, not everyone is like him, tell him that.

A I'll tell him ... Sir. [*exits*]

Z What if he won't give me something to eat? Maybe I should sell these trousers. No, better to starve and arrive home in Saratov in my St. Petersburg suit. I wish Osip hadn't stopped me from hiring that carriage. I could've made my entrance into town in it, dropping in on some ghastly neighbor with Osip in back dressed in livery. [*playing Osip*] "Ivan Alexandrovich Khlestakov requests admittance." They wouldn't even know what "requests admittance" means. When they enter a home they just barge into the parlor like a bunch of bears. But as for me, I approach the pretty little daughter of the house and say, "Lovely maiden, I am so so ..." Dammit, I'm so hungry I could eat a horse.

A, as waiter, enters with tray and cover.

A The manager says that this is your last supper.

Z Manager? I spit on the manager.

Z immediately lifts the cover and spits into the soup.

A Soup and roast chicken … Sir.

Z I spit on your soup. Only two dishes?

A Two … Sir.

Z eats the soup hungrily.

Z I refuse to eat this. This is revolting. Tell him that this will not do. Too little.

A The manager says that it is too much.

Z Where's the sauce for the chicken?

A There is no sauce … Sir.

Z And why not? Earlier I passed the kitchen myself. There was plenty of sauce. And there were two weird little men in the dining room this morning stuffing themselves on an enormous pink salmon.

A Well, Sir ... we do have sauce ... but we don't have sauce.

Z You do and you don't?

A Yes. No.

Z And salmon? Fish? Cutlets? Yes? No?

A Yes. For our superior guests. Sir.

Z You numbskull.

A Yes ... Sir.

Z Why do they eat and not me?

A There's a difference ... Sir.

Z What difference?

A They pay ... Sir.

Z I'm wasting my breath on a birdbrain like you. What's this soup, anyway? There is no soup here. They just poured water into a dirty pot. It's got no taste at all. It just stinks of greasy dishes. Bring me another. [*A starts to exit.*] Leave the tray here, nitwit. [*Z picks up the chicken.*] Ai, ai, ai, you call this a chicken?

A Then what is it?

Z Who knows? [*Z eats the chicken.*] You're all phonies around here, every last one of you. Fancy giving people rubbish like this. It's criminal! One bite and you choke to death. This skin is like birch bark. Swindlers. [*A exits.*] Tell the manager that I will report him to the mayor! My God, they don't know the first thing about hospitality. If I had some loose change, I could send Osip out to the market to get me a bun. Who does he think he is anyway, this hotel manager? What am I, some traveling salesman or shopkeeper or common laborer? [*A enters as mayor.*] I'll tell him to his face, "How dare you!" I'll say, "Who do you think you are?" I'll say. "Who the hell are you?"

Z sees him. They are terrified of each other.

A I have the honor ... to greet you.

Z Oh, how do you do?

A Pardon me.

Z Oh no, the pardon is all mine.

A It is my duty, as the authority in this town ...

Z Duty?

A Uh, yes ... I do have a duty ... to ensure that all personages passing through suffer ...

Z Suffer?

A Yes ... suffer no oppressive circumstances.

Z But it wasn't my fault. I will pay. The money is coming from my village. The manager here is to blame. He serves chicken that tastes like a sweaty pillow. And the soup—God only knows what he puts in the soup—I had to throw it out the window just now. He is starving me to death with his filthy food. So, what could I do?

A Forgive me. Our market sells only the most superior quality chickens. I haven't a clue as to where he gets his chickens. And if everything is not to your liking here, permit me to accompany you to more ... private quarters.

Z No, I won't go. I know what your private quarters are. The jailhouse. What gives you the right? How dare you? I serve the government ... in St. Petersburg!

A Oh my God.

Z I will not leave this hotel. I'll go straight to the Ministry.

A Have mercy, don't destroy me. I have a wife and a daughter.

Z ...You have a wife ... and a daughter?

A Yes. Besides, they pay me almost nothing here. Look. [*reaches into his pocket*] A pittance. Not even enough to keep me in tea and sugar. And, if there have ever been tiny little bribes here and there, it only amounts to a mere trifle for the table or a strip of cloth for a dress. And as for the sergeant's wife who got herself beaten up ...

Z Beaten up? Please, no. I will pay, I swear. I just don't have anything on me right now.

A If it is only that you are in need of money, then I am at your service.

Z Uh ... yes, lend me ... lend me a little. Oh, not much, say, something in the order of two hundred rubles, or even a bit less.

A [*handing him a bundle of notes*] No need to count, it's exactly two hundred.

Z Much obliged. [*He stuffs the money in his pocket.*]

A Sit down, I beg you.

Z No, I prefer to stand.

A Please, Sir, sit down. Sit ... down. You see, I am not your ordinary, garden-variety type of mayor. Next to my duty to my townspeople, there is my feeling for all humanity. And so, I wish to serve you, Sir, as best as I can. This being the case, I just happened by the hotel, you know, to see how those passing through our town are being looked after.

Z The pleasure is all mine, I'm sure. If you hadn't come, I would not have been able to pay my way out of here.

A [*as an aside*] Listen to him, "wouldn't be able." [*to Z*] Now, may I be so boldfaced as to enquire where you are heading?

Z I'm off home, old chap. To my estate in Saratov.

A Saratov. [*as an aside*] And he doesn't even blush, making us think that he is a lowly official. I'm going to have to watch this one. Puny, nasty-looking runt of a man. [*to Z*] You have a lovely trip before you. Travel certainly is an enriching experience. Or have you come to be enriched in other ways?

Z Well, my uncle's making me go home. He's angry because I haven't been promoted yet. He thinks they pin a medal in your lapel the moment you get there. Wish I could pack him off to my office for a day.

A [*aside*] Imagine, dragging his uncle into the story. [*to Z*] And is this journey of yours an extensive one?

Z Don't know, to tell you the truth. The old geezer's as dumb as a mule ... and as stubborn. I'm going to tell him straight out: I can't live anywhere but Petersburg. What am I supposed to do, waste my life among peasants? My soul is starving for enlightenment.

A [*aside*] Lying through his teeth. But a pretty clever story. [*to Z*] Your remarks are so true. How can a man live in the middle of nowhere? Take me, for instance. Never sleep, suffer for the homeland, never regret anything, and who knows when I will get my due rewards? Does this room seem a wee bit cramped for you?

Z Cramped? Oh yes. The bedbugs here bite like bulldogs.

A Such an important guest should not be made to suffer because of mere bedbugs. And isn't it a trifle dark in here for you?

Z Dark? Oh yes. Very very dark. The manager here won't even spare me a candle. Now and then one aches for a good read, or the fantasy overcomes one to compose something ... or other. But one cannot, because it's too dark.

A You shouldn't be here.

Z I shouldn't?

A No. You should be somewhere else.

Z Somewhere else?

A Yes. I have a room for you. Lovely room. Light and quiet. But, no, it would be too great an honor.

Z For whom?

A For me. Do not be cross with me. I only ask out of a simple heart.

Make me a happy man. Stay at my home. My wife would be delighted. My daughter would be delighted.

They embrace, cheek to cheek.

Z I am indebted to you. We are two of a kind. I, like you, despise two-faced people. I greatly appreciate your sincerity and cordiality. I ask for nothing more in life than loyalty and respect. And I am very anxious to meet your wife ... and your daughter.

A And perhaps you would like ... to inspect?

Z Inspect? What do you mean by inspect?

A Would Your Honor perhaps care to look over some of our public buildings, I wonder?

Z Whatever for?

A Why, to see how we do things here, how the town is kept in order and so on and so forth.

Z Well, all right, if you like.

A If you wish, we could inspect the local school, see how our children are taught there.

Z Sure, fine, fine.

A And then, if you so desire, we could stop in at the police station and visit our local lock-up, observe how we, uh, lock up our criminals.

Z Why the lock-up? I'd much rather observe ... the hospital.

A As you wish. And how shall we go? In your own carriage or mine?

Z Oh, I think I'd rather go in yours. What's this? What's this paper?

A Why, it's your hotel bill. Do not worry, though. No need to pay.

Z I will write a note to your wife and daughter. [*Z writes on the bill.*]

A They will swoon over your very words.

Z I hope so.

They smile at each other. Fade to blackout.
The lights come up on the mayor's living room.

Scene change—mayor's living room.

Z enters wearing a hunting hat with feather. He surveys the room, singing a Russian song. He sits on the sofa. He finds the drawer in it and opens it, taking out the bottle of vodka. He takes a swig.

Z Oi, oi, oi, my head's spinning from all that vodka they gave me during my "inspections." Still, I think I'm going to like it here. They certainly know how to treat visitors. Yes, I think I could get used to living in a place like this.

He does not hear A enter. A is now Anna, the mayor's wife.

A Good afternoon.

Z [*bolting up*] Good afternoon.

A I received your note.

Z I am embarrassed to write such drivel to a woman of your beauty.

A Drivel? This is sheer poetry. "My darling, though we have never met, two portions of smoked salmon, caviar, pickled cucumbers..."

Z That's, uh, the hotel bill.

They both laugh.

A Oh, but … "My darling...."

Z Well, you see, I do toss off poems on the odd occasion. How happy I am, Madame, to possess the pleasure of seeing you.

A Meeting a man of your ... stature ... is an even greater pleasure.

Z Please, Madame, on the contrary, my pleasure is far, far bigger.

A Can that be so? You flatter me dead. Won't you please sit down?

Z To stand beside you is my deepest happiness. However, if you insist, I will sit. [*They sit together on the sofa.*] Ah, what happiness it is for me to be finally sitting beside you.

A I dare not believe that you could be talking about me. I dare not think your words are anything but sheer politeness, Sir. I imagine that such a sojourn must be very tedious to you, living in the capital, as you do.

Z Oh, an extreme tediosity, Madame. When one is accustomed, comprenny-vous, to life in the highest society, suddenly to find myself on the road, living in filthy inns amidst the gloom of ignorance. If it weren't for today's happy turn of events ... [*looking up into Anna's eyes*] ... which I assure you make up for everything.

A It must all be so very unpleasant for you, Sir.

Z At this moment, Madame, I am feeling very pleasant.

A Oh, how can you say such things! You honor me, and I am not worthy of you.

Z No, Madame, you are worthy. So very worthy.

A But I am only a country girl.

Z But the country has its little hills ... and brooks. Of course, it is nothing like the capital. The chief of my section and I are like this. He comes up to me, slaps me on the shoulder and says, he says, he says, "Well, let's have lunch."

A He does?

Z Oh yes. Just like that. And I stick my head into where the pretty secretaries are working and I say, I say, "Keep up the good work."

A You do?

Z Oh yes. And then, while at lunch, I write a bit, or meet a few of the great writers. Me and Dostoevsky, for instance, are just like this.

A You are?

Z Oh yes. I say to him, I say, I say, "Fyodor, how's tricks?" And you know what he answers?

A No.

Z He says, he says, "Not bad, not bad." That Dostoevsky, what a joker! And I've written a few books myself, you know. "War and Peace," "The Brothers Kerosenov." I wrote Goethe's "Faust," you know. So many, I can't even recall all the titles. Not that I wanted to write the stuff in the first place. It's the theater directors. They implore me, "Please, please write us something." So, I think, "What the hell," and by the next morning the whole thing's written and they're bowled over by it. It all just comes into my mind and right out again. Everything written by Dr. Zhivago ... it's all by me.

A You're Dr. Zhivago?

Z Well, I proofread all his articles and I taste his medicines for him.

The doorbell rings.

A Oh, I must go. My husband has returned! [*at the door*] Zhivago!

Z Me?

A Zhivago....

A exits. Z helps himself to more vodka, then takes a cushion and dances with it, getting increasingly excited. He whispers in the cushion's ear, strokes it, sighs, throws it down on the sofa, touches it all over, and mounts it.

A, as the mayor, enters.

A Is everything to your liking?

Z Oh yes! No complaints. Wonderful institutions. I like the way you show off your town to visitors. No one ever showed me a thing in the other dumps I've been in.

A I'm afraid that in your average town the officials are preoccupied with their own profits. Whereas, in my town, my sole thought is how to be vigilant and gain the approval of superiors.

Z That meal we had was superb. I literally ate like a pig. You eat like that every day, do you?

A Only when we have such important guests.

Z I like a good meal. Yes, what is life for if not to pluck the flowers of pleasure? Where was it we ate again? The hospital, was it?

A That's right, the hospital.

Z Oh yes, I recall there being beds around. And have all your patients recovered then? There didn't seem to be many about.

A Only about a handful left, no more. The rest are … gone. Since I took the reins here, the patients have been recovering like flies. They barely manage to set foot in the hospital and, bang! … they're better. It's not so much the medicines as the honest and orderly administration. Most mayors, I tell you, only care about feathering their own nest. But all I ever ask, as I rest my weary head on my pillow at night, is that those people higher up look down on me with favor for my zealousness. When the whole town is kept down in law and order, the streets clean, the prisoners locked down, or up, drunkards safely out-of-sight … what more can I ask? I desire no honors. What are honors compared to a life of good deeds? Merely ashes and vaingloriousness.

Z True, true. I must confess, I enjoy dallying in philosophy, too, writing the odd prose piece or tossing off the occasional poem. But tell me, please, haven't you other diversions here, spots where a man might, strictly for argument's sake, indulge in a game of cards?

A God forbid! I have never heard of such things here. These fingers have never held so much as a single card in them. Wouldn't even recognize one if they saw it. And if I did catch myself even so much as glimpsing those kings of diamonds or whatever they're called, it would make me sick. Sick! A disgusting way to kill precious government time, if you ask me.

Z Yes, sure. Nice place you have here. I myself have my own little abode in St. Petersburg, everyone knows it. Just ask: "Where's the little abode of Ivan Alexandrovich?" If you are passing through the capital, do stop by. I throw the most lavish parties.

A They must be luxurious indeed.

Z You've no conception. On the table, for instance, there might be a watermelon worth seven hundred rubles. The soup could be fresh off the steamer from gay Paree. You lift the lid and the French steam hits you right in the face. And there's always a card game going. Four of us: the Minister of Foreign Affairs, the French Ambassador, the English Ambassador, the German Ambassador ... and me. And at work, well, once I was head of my whole section. The director disappeared and never came back. I took over his job and went through the place like an earthquake, really shook them all up. Yes, they trembled like dead leaves about to fall. Oh, it's no joke. Even the Privy Council shakes in their boots when I'm around. And why? Because I tell them, "I know myself. Myself!" I am everywhere, everywhere. I'm in the palace every day. And tomorrow? Tomorrow they're going to make me a Field Marshal!

A [*terrified*] Your ... you r... ex ...

Z What are you trying to say?

A Yo-ur lexency ... Exclensy ... I think I know what it is you really desire most.

Z You do?

A Yes. You desire to be treated well ...

Z ... yes? ...

A ... and sent on your way.

Z You are a man of great wisdom.

A Thank you.

Z Don't mention it.

A That's right, please lie down. Make yourself comfortable. After all, what's mine is yours, as they say. You know what else they say? "A bird who flies from nest to nest does not mind taking a drink out of another bird's bath." Here's a few rubles for your next bath.

Z [*grabbing the money*] Thank you.

A Don't mention it. And here's something to dry yourself off with.

Z [*grabbing the money*] Thank you.

A I am so pleased. You see, I know that the townspeople are also pleased that you have come all the way out here to see us. They are, shall I say, concerned that you have a favorable impression of our town. We wouldn't want people to know, I mean, to think ...

A exits. The door gradually opens. It is A dressed as Bobchinsky.

A Sir, may I have the great pleasure to introduce myself: Pyotr Ivanovich Bobchinsky, director of our postal services.

Z Pleased, I'm sure. Be seated. You live here, do you?

A Yessir.

Z I like this little town you've got here, you know. Of course, you don't have many people here, but, really, it's not the capital, is it. That's true, isn't it? It's not the capital, is it.

A Absolutely true, Sir.

Z Indeed, it's only in the capital that one finds the high society, and not a bunch of hicks. What is your opinion on that, eh?

A Absolutely true, Sir. [*aside*] He's so open about everything. And so curious to know what I think.

Z Now, come clean with me. Is it possible to live a happy life in such a little town like this?

A Absolutely, Sir.

Z What do people need, I ask myself. They need only to be respected and genuinely loved. Isn't that so?

A Totally so, Sir.

Z I'm delighted, I must confess, that you share my opinions. Some, needless to say, think me odd, but, well, I am who I am. [*to himself*] I wonder if I can hit him for a loan. [*to A*] You know, the strangest thing happened to me. I was … detained on the way here. You couldn't by any chance lend me three hundred rubles, could you?

A But of course. Nothing would give me greater pleasure. Here you are, Sir. I am happy to serve you from the bottom of my soul.

Z Much obliged. You see, I must confess, I'd rather die than deprive myself while on the road. I mean, why should I, eh? Don't you agree?

A Absolutely, Sir. Just one thing, if I may make a humble request. When you get back to St. Petersburg, tell all the important people there, all the senators and admirals, tell them that in a certain town lives Pyotr Ivanovich Bobchinsky. Just say, "Pyotr Ivanovich Bobchinsky lives."

Z Very well.

A And if you should happen to meet the Tsar, say to him, "Your Imperial Majesty, in a certain little town there is a Pyotr Ivanovich Bobchinsky."

Z Very well.

A Now, I won't disturb you further with my presence. Would you have any instructions for me as to the running of the postal services?

Z No, nothing. [*A exits*] Postmaster seems to be a decent sort of fellow, too. Obliging, at least. I love people like that.

A returns as Dr. Lapkin-Flapkin, the town doctor.

A Sir, it gives me great pleasure to introduce myself: Director of Healthy Services, Dr. Lapkin-Flapkin. I had the immense honor of receiving you at the hospital.

Z So you did. I remember. That was an excellent meal you provided me with.

A I am happy to put myself out in the service of my country.

Z Good food is, I confess, a weakness of mine. You know, it seems to me that you were a bit shorter before lunch.

A That's quite possible. I never spare myself, Sir, in my passion for serving the state. Which is more than can be said for others. The postmaster here, for instance, never does a stroke of work. The post office itself is neglected, the mails are held up for days on end. And the judge! His behavior—and I say this solely in the interests of our country, for he is an acquaintance and a relative of mine—his behavior is reprehensible.

Z Is that a fact?

A There's a landowner here, Dobchinsky, whom I believe you saw at the hotel. Soon as Dobchinsky leaves his house, the judge takes Dobchinsky's place beside Dobchinsky's wife. I swear. Look at Dobchinsky's children. Not one of them looks like Dobchinsky. Every one of them, even the little girl, is the spitting image of the judge.

Z You don't say. Who would have thought it?

A And the school principal … I've no idea how he got appointed. He's worse than an anarchist, and it's impossible to describe how unruly his, uh, rules are. I am prepared, if you wish, to put this all down on paper.

Z Good, why not? I enjoy reading amusing things when I'm bored stiff. Now tell me, what was your name again?

A Dr. Lapkin-Flapkin.

Z Ah yes, Lapkin-Flapkin.

A Now, I dare not trouble you any further and take up time from your valuable duties.

Z It's nothing, I assure you. It's all been most amusing, what you've told me. Come again. I love this sort of thing. Oh, but yes, just one thing. The damnedest thing happened to me. I've been cleared out of cash, cleared right out. I suppose you couldn't lend me, say four hundred?

A [*reluctantly*] Of course. Here you are: two ... three ... four ... hundred.

Z Thank you, so much, my dear doctor.

A exits. Z counts his money. A enters as Judge Luka Lukich Khlopov.

A I have the honor of introducing myself: Luka Lukich Khlopov, Judge of the District Court.

Z So you're the judge here? I see. Quite a lucrative position, I suspect. What is that in your hand?

A This? Oh, nothing much.

Z What do you mean nothing much. Oh, you have dropped some money.

A Money? [*aside*] Oh God, I'm halfway to Siberia.

Z What was that? Why yes, it's money.

A Well ... it kind of fell out of my hands ... it ...

Z Give it to me as a loan.

A A loan? Why yes, with pleasure.

Z I spent all my money on the road, you know. I'll send this back to you as soon as I reach my home village.

A This is an honor for me. And don't believe the lies they tell about me. Why, just the other day, the sergeant's wife came in beaten to a pulp, and I really threw the book at her for daring to appear before me in such a shocking state. [*knock at door*]. Ah, it must be the director of our educational services. Do you have any instructions for me, Sir?

Z Instructions? What kind of instructions?

A For the district court?

Z Good God, no.

A Then I dare not trouble you further with my presence.

Z Goodbye.

A exits. A enters as the teacher, appearing very nervous. He goes directly to Z, hands him some money and exits.

Z He seems quite a decent fellow.

A re-enters, again as teacher.

A Sir, I love my pupils. So much so that I keep some of them in school for years.

Z Look, sit down, will you? Sit down. Have a cigar.

A Oh God, do I take it or don't I?

Z These aren't bad at all. They can't hold a candle to the ones in St. Petersburg, of course. Here's a light. Light up. That's the wrong end, professor. [*A drops the cigar.*] It's obvious you're no connoisseur of cigars.

A [*to himself*] Oh God, I'm ruined now.

Z A good cigar is my weakness, I must confess. And, my other weakness is for the female sex. What about you? Which do you fancy, brunettes or blondes? No, tell me frankly, brunettes or blondes?

A I don't dare venture to have an opinion, Sir.

Z No, no, come on, don't prevaricate. I want to know your honest preference.

A I'd venture to say ... may I be so bold to suggest ... Oh God what am I talking about?

Z Ah. Ah! You don't want to tell me. I bet some brunette's got you wound around her little finger, eh? Admit it, she does, doesn't she.

A Well, your excellent, uh, ex-cellency, I am awed by ...

Z Awed? Yes, I do inspire awe in people. At least, I know, there isn't a single woman who could resist me. Wouldn't you say?

A Absolutely, Sir. Now, I must not disgrace you any longer with my presence. Except to say … to say … to say …

Z Goodbye.

A exits.

Z The people in this town, the mayor included, seem to have taken me for someone from the government, an inspector or something. What idiots! I must write Trapkin in St. Petersburg about this. [*He writes a letter.*] He'll get a good play out of this. No, no one would believe it: three hundred from the postmaster, four hundred from the doctor, five hundred from the teacher, and three hundred from the judge … five hundred, seven fifty, nine fifty … fifteen hundred rubles. What a reception!

A, as Osip, enters. Z continues to write the letter.

Z Osip, Osip, you won't believe this. The officials in this town seem to have taken me for someone from the government, an inspector or something. What fools! I'm writing Trapkin in St. Petersburg about it all.

A Yes, but one thing.

Z What?

A We must get out of here. It's time to leave.

Z Leave? Ridiculous. Why?

A We've lolled around here for too long already.

Z No, I feel like staying a bit longer. We'll go tomorrow.

A Tomorrow? Let's go now while we can. Besides, your uncle in Saratov will flip his lid over your taking so long to get home. We could be out of here in a flash ... with the money.

Z Very well. But take this letter to the post office first and tell them to send it urgently to St. Petersburg. Oh, dammit, I can't remember Trapkin's address. Oh yes. "Post Office Street." [*Osip exits.*] He'll die laughing when he reads this. [*yelling offstage*] And tell the postmaster that it's on government business so it won't need a stamp!

There is a pounding on the door. Z counts his money. A's voice as Chang from offstage.

A Let me in. Please, Your Honor. Let me in.

Z Come in.

A enters as Chang, the clothier.

A Sir, I must talk with you.

Z All right, talk. Do you have something for me?

A Yes, a petition.

Z A petition? [*He takes the petition and reads it.*] "To the Keeper of the National Treasury, from the clothier Chang." There is no such title as Keeper of the National Treasury. Is that all?

A We are suffering in this town.

Z At whose hands?

A The mayor's. He takes me by the neck and hollers, "You lousy Tatar," and though I've always done what is expected of me and showered his wife and daughter with dresses from my business, he just walks into my shop and grabs whatever he likes and says, "Hey, boy, nice piece of cloth you got here, send it around to my house." No joke, it's a fifty-meter roll of my best material.

Z Really? The swindler. He ought to be packed right off to Siberia.

A Wherever Your Excellency wishes to send him isn't far enough away for us. Now, kind Sire, please accept my most humble offering: some sugar and a skin of wine.

Z Do you think that I would take any sort of bribe? If, however, for argument's sake, you proposed to lend me, say, the odd three hundred rubles, that would be a different story. Loans I can accept.

A Please allow me, Sire. Better you should have five hundred.

Z A loan.

A And some sugar as well.

Z No bribes.

There is a pounding at the door.

A Oh my God, that could be the mayor.

A rushes out by the side. Z counts the new money and tosses the petition aside. Again we hear a voice from offstage: "Let me in, Your Worship, I must talk to you! I must have an audience with you! Please let me in!"

Z Enter, please.

A enters as the baker.

A Please do not destroy me. I have done nothing wrong, I ... I ...

Z All right, I won't.

A It's all the mayor's fault. Whenever he comes into my bakery I have to hide my cakes. He puts his fingers into any old rubbish that we sell. Eclairs that have been sitting on the shelf for seven months that not even a delivery boy's horse would eat, the mayor grabs and devours in one gulp. He makes me bake a cake for his birthday and then six months later has another birthday and I have to bake another cake for him.

Z is searching A's pockets for money, getting flour on him.

Z He's a common thief, that's all there is to it. Look, I never take bribes. But if you could lend me, say, just for argument's sake, this money, I could find it in my heart to accept it.

A By all means. [*from under his hat*] And here's another three hundred. So long as you punish the mayor for me. [*exits*]

Z I will. I will. Amazing. They hate him, they really hate him.

A's voice as the sergeant's wife is heard outside the room. "Let me in. please, kind sir, I must see you. Let me in!"

Z Oh, do come in. Is it Anna? Or is it Márya? Whichever, they are so so eager to please.

Z *combs his hair, fixes his shirt. The door opens. A enters as the sergeant's wife.*

A Oh.

Z Ah.

A Oh.

Z Ah. What can you do for me?

A I beg you.

Z [*to audience*] That's a good start.

A I am the sergeant's wife.

Z Did he do this to you? You look so … bruised.

A It's the mayor's fault. He forced my husband to join the army.

Z Did he do that? The brute.

A I hope he decomposes in daylight and his maiden aunt with him and if his father's still alive I hope he dies or chokes to death on a mouthful of dirt. "What do you want a husband for anyway?" he tells me. "He's no good to you anymore."

Z I see.

A Then he says, "Your husband's a thief, and even if he isn't one, he could be," so he sends him away to the army to stop him from stealing. How can I go on without a husband?

Z I was thinking the very same thing.

A I am a weak woman.

Z Oh.

A I hope his mother-in-law croaks on top of a cliff. And if not his mother-in-law, then his father-in-law, and if not his ...

Z All right, all right. Calm down, calm down. Shhh.

A And then he had me flogged.

Z The mayor did this to you?

A I couldn't sit down for two days.

Z Ah. But what can I do about that?

A You could make it better.

Z I could?

A Yes. You could make him pay for his mistake. I would be forever in your hands.

Z Oh.

A Ah.

Z puts his hand to A's cheek. A bites it playfully, but hard.

Z Ahhhhhh!

A smiles and leaves. Z nurses his hand. He stuffs his money into his pockets. A as Márya enters, calling to him. He hides.

A Zhivago. Oh, Dr. Zhivago!

Z [*from behind*] Did I startle you, dear? Where are you going?

A Going? I was just wondering if mama was in here. I've disturbed you. You have such important matters on your mind.

Z Your eyes are much more important than any important matters. You could never disturb me. Au contraire, you bring me pleasure. Oui, oui.

A You have such a way with words.

Z There are no words to describe an exquisite creature such as you. Please sit down. You deserve not a sofa, but a throne.

A [*sitting*] No, really, I must be going.

Z What a beautiful shawl you have on.

A You are making fun of us provincials with your elegant jibes.

Z How I would love to be your shawl so that I might embrace your lily neck.

A I do not fully comprehend your words. My shawl? How can ...

what strange, hot weather we're having today.

Z Your lips are hotter than any weather.

A The things you say. I wanted to ask you to write some verses for me in my album. You must know so many verses.

Z For you, anything your breast desires. Verses?

A Yes, any verses, really. Something original.

Z Well, yes, I know so many original verses. All right. "Shall I compare thee to a winter's tale...." Is that nice? But I would rather declare my love for you than spout a poem, for, from the moment I laid ... eyes on you, I ...

A Love? I do not fully understand. I never really know what people mean by love.

Z Why do you move away from me? We should be close to each other.

A Close? Just the same if we are ... not so close.

Z Just the same if we are not so far.

A I do not ... fully ...

Z You see, it only appears to you that we are close. Imagine that we are far, far apart. Darling, I would be so happy if I could take you ...

A Oh, what's that? A bird just flew by the window, a magpie, or a ...

Z [*kissing her shoulder*] A magpie ...

A ... or a ... no, you have gone too far. Out of the blue like ... like ...

Z I do it out of love, only out of love. Forgive me.

A You take me for some easy hick or something. [*exits*]

Z Love, do not be cross. I stand on my knees and beg your forgiveness. Forgive me. Forgive me. I am on my knees. Look at me.

Z sings a love song. A enters as Anna.

A Well, this is a surprise. What does this mean, Sir?

Z Oh, Anna, dear Anna. I beg you.

A Please stand up. The floor is so dirty.

Z No, I am on my knees. I must know what my destiny is to be. Life or death.

A If I am not mistaken, you have made advances toward my daughter.

Z No, it is you I love. My life is hanging by a hair. I do not deserve to crawl on the earth under your feet. Darling, with a flaming breast, I ask for your hand.

A Permit me to point out that, well, um, I am already married, in a manner of speaking.

A disappears behind the sofa.

Z Think nothing of it. Love recognizes no mere legalities. Come with me and make haste now to a brady shook ... shady brook. Marry me. Marry me. I can whisk you out of this miserable existence into a world of beauty and power. I can show you a life that no one in this hole can dream of.

Z makes love to her, though we do not see her, just hear the noises as articles of clothing are tossed over the back of the sofa.

Z I can make you happy, as I am about to do this very moment. I must be allowed to show you what kind of a man I am. Compared to that weak, impotent, puffed-up toady husband of yours who makes the sounds of a man but displays the actions of a consummate, ineffectual twit, I am a man, a real man who can take his wife to the cleaners ... [*A's head, as the mayor, appears from the wings. Z notices A.*] ... excellent cleaners in this town, you know, I ...

A Have you seen my wife?

Z Your ...? She is under ... under ... standably not here, I mean, elsewhere ... ooooo....

A You can't trust anybody these days, not even your own wife. [*A pulls in his head.*]

Z Absolutely. Oh, darling, your little hands are so freezing. [*singing*] Che gelida manina! Ooooo ... I do love you, I adore you ... you will take me to heaven, and from heaven I will go directly to Saratov ... oh, my God, this is unbelievable, never have I known a woman such as you.

Z, on top of "Anna," is in ecstasy. A, as Márya, enters from the side.

A Mama? Mama? I thought I heard mama in here with you.

Z [*immediately falling over the sofa and, pants down, crawling to her*] No, it is you. Life or death, you must decide for me. I want to make you my little bride.

A swoons. Z lifts her and puts her on the sofa, saying "Excuse me" to "Anna."

Z Oh my God, now I have you both where I want you. I love you, I love you both. I will have you both together, mother and daughter. You will both be my brides. Big Bride and … Slightly Smaller Bride. I can handle it. I can possess you both right now, not like that old fart of a husband and father you have, the kind of man who is crude, who does not know how to treat women properly, the kind of man who can never … never …

A as the mayor enters.

Z … never in my life have I had such a marvelous reception. Thank you for everything, Mayor.

Z jumps up and, pants at his knees, tries to keep A away from the sofa.

A Don't believe them, please don't believe them.

Z Don't believe them? Don't believe who?

A The people in this town are all liars, cheats.

Z Aw, I know that.

A Do not ruin me. Everybody in this town knows what frauds the shopkeepers ... you do?

Z Sure. Liars and cheats, down to the very last man. Now ... over here, please. This is in the strictest confidence. Not that way. Here, here.

A The sergeant's wife told you a pack of lies.

Z Of course she did.

A If she says I beat her up, she's lying. She beat herself up.

Z Of course she did.

A She did?

Z It goes without saying. Now, you must give her to me.

A Give her to you? But she is already given.

Z That makes no difference to me.

A It doesn't? Well, I suppose, her husband is in the army....

Z Not the sergeant's wife. I had someone a bit closer to home in mind, Mayor.

A Closer to home?

Z Uh-huh.

A This home?

Z Uh-huh.

A My ... ?

Z Your ...

A Daughter?

Z I must have her.

A Have her?

Z Yes. I am a desperate man. If I shoot myself in the head, you will be the cause of it. You will be sent up for murder.

A I'm not guilty, I swear. Don't be angry with me. I will do anything for you.

Z I want to marry your daughter.

A Agreed.

Z Then bless us quick.

A I bless you, my son.

Z Thank you. Not so loud. The walls have ears.

They shake hands.

A This calls for a toast. I have some vodka in the sofa and we ...

Z No, not the sofa!

A Eh?

Z No. I do not drink. Not during the day, that is. Vodka kept in a sofa is … no good.

A Then I will make the arrangements for the wedding. Leave it to me. Leave everything to me … son.

Z All right, I'll be off, then.

A Off? You're leaving?

Z Yes. Leaving.

A But you yourself were just alluding about a, well, wedding.

Z Oh, it'll only be for a minute, I mean, a day. To see my uncle. He's very rich and very old.

A We wouldn't ever presume to hold you back, and we look forward to your speedy recovery here.

Z Oh yes, before you know it.

A Do you, perhaps, require something? Weren't you a trifle short of cash?

Z No, no. What could have made you think that? … Yes, well, as you wish.

A How much would you like?

Z Well, you gave me two hundred before, that is, not exactly two, it was more like four hundred. I mustn't take advantage of your miscalculation, must I? So, if you could let me have, say, the same again, it would sort of round it out.

A It's yours. [*He produces the money.*] There, all crisp new notes.

Z So they are. [*He takes and examines the notes.*] Perfect. Don't they say, "Fresh notes bring fresh happiness?"

A They do, they do.

Z Well, goodbye then, Anton Antonovich. I am obliged to you for all your hospitality. I must confess, from the bottom of my heart, I have never been so well received ... anywhere.

Z exits. A picks up a phone.

A I'll fix those sycophants with their entreaties and petitions. Ivan Karpovich. Get the shopkeepers in to see me. Complain about me, will they? Damn Judases. They're going to be begging for mercy before I get through with them. I want a list of every damn one of them who said a word against me, everyone who signed a petition. And make sure that everybody in town hears of the honor that has befallen the mayor, that he is giving his daughter away in marriage not to some provincial clod, but to a rare bird of a man, a man capable of anything. Anything, dammit! I want everybody to know. Scream it out, ring the bloody bells, dammit. A celebration must sound like a celebration!

Z enters as Bobchinsky.

Z I have the honor to congratulate you and wish you a long life and the blessings of prosperity, Anton Antonovich.

A Thank you, Bobchinsky.

Z But tell me how it all happened?

A I'm bound to be promoted. He rubs shoulders with ministers, ambassadors. I could creep up and up.

Z Yes, you could.

A I'm not marrying my daughter off to some imbecile like you, thank God.

Z Yes, thank God. But how did it happen, Anton Antonovich?

A Well, it was extraordinary. He proposed to her entirely of his own free will. It was love at first sight. "Anna, darling," he said ... I just happened to overhear some of it. "Anna, darling, I love you."

Z But Anna is your wife.

A Ah. "Márya, darling," he said, "Márya, darling, I love you. Your many charms are my aspirations. I have the utmost respect for your qualifications." It was so ... lofty. I said to him, "Sir, this is much too great an honor to bestow on people like us," but he says, he says, on his hands and knees, he says, "Ann ..." ... I mean, "Márya, do not make me an unhappy man. If you say no, I will end my life in death."

Z Beautiful.

A "I'll shoot myself. I'll shoot myself."

Z Mayor ...

A Not me, nitwit, him. He'll shoot himself.

Z Beautiful.

A I think so. It comes as just deserts for my long service to my country.

Z Where is he now?

A Oh, he's just left for a day or two. On important business. To get his uncle's blessing.

Z Let us toast your good fortune. May the devil take you.

A Thank you. Same to you.

They drink. Z pours another drink for the two of them.

Z Beautiful.

A Same to you.

They drink. Z pours two shots, says vashe zdorovye and downs them both.

Z Oh, I almost forgot. I found this letter at the post office.

A What do you mean, found?

Z Well, it was written by him himself.

A Who?

Z   Your new son-in-law. I glimpsed the address and I see, "Post Office Street." So, I think to myself, I think, "Uh-oh, he found something wrong with the post office here and he is informing on me to the capital." Then I feel this unnatural force forcing me to open the letter. I can't do it. I can't. I can. I can. Yes, no. Yes, no. Open, don't open, open ...

A   Give me that letter.

Z   One voice telling me, "If you don't open it, your head will be twisted off like a chicken's," another saying, "If you open it, your head will be twisted off like a chicken's." I was trembling. I felt giddy inside. I opened it.

A   You dared open a letter of such an important man?

Z   But he isn't an important man.

A   My future son-in-law, not important?

Z   Yes. No.

A   What is he then, eh? How dare you call him anything but important. I place you under arrest. [*He goes to the phone again.*]

Z   Do you? [*reading the letter*] "I hasten to inform you, my dear Trapkin, the miracles I am presently living through."

A   You see? Miracles. [*dials, but misdials, half listens*]

Z   "On the road I lost my shirt in a game with some captain or other, and when I arrived here the hotel manager wanted to throw me in jail for not paying. But then, due to my St. Petersburg appearance, the whole town took me for an inspector or somebody. [*A puts the phone down.*] And now I'm living in the mayor's own house, high on the hog with his daughter and wife. The only trouble is, I can't decide which to start on first. I think I'll have a go at the old lady. She looks as if she's ready for anything. Besides, everybody here gives me all the loans I want. They're such simpletons! You'd die laughing. First there's the mayor, as thick as a donkey's ass." Shall I go on?

A That's not what it says.

Z Read it yourself.

A "Thick as a donkey's ... "

Z " ... ass."

A Ah.

Z Hmmm, let's see. "Donkey's ass, donkey's ass" ... oh, here. "The man in the post office is ... " It's nothing. It's sort of illegible here.

A " ... in the post office is a stupid dolt who guzzles vodka for breakfast ... the doctor looks just like a pig in a wig; the judge thinks about his dogs so much he's beginning to look like one; the teacher can't talk for twitching. Otherwise, all in all, one must say, they are a generous, good-natured lot. Well, goodbye, dear Trapkin. Life is dull, unless someone like a playwright gives us food for our soul." It's addressed to Ivan Vasilievich Trapkin, 97 Post Office Street, Turn Through the Courtyard, 3rd floor, 1st Door on Your Right, St. Petersburg. He has killed me. Killed me. I cannot see anything. I see only pigs' snouts where there should be faces. I can't see anything else. Get him back here. Get him back here!

Z   How? He's gone from here. [*exiting*] Not even the fastest troika could catch up with him now. [*taking the bottle with him, exits*]

A   All that money. How could I be such a fool? Thirty years I have been a politician, and no one has ever gotten the better of me. I've swindled the most cunning opponents. I've hoodwinked three governors, not that governors are anything really. And now he is engaged to my own daughter. Well, no daughter of mine.... Oh, you idiot, you fat-nosed fool, to take that puny little runt for a man of power! Now he's on his way, telling his story to half the world. And what's worse, some scribbler will write a damn play about it, some starving little nobody playwright! They'll exaggerate the truth and everyone will grin and clap their hands. Who are you laughing at, eh? Who? You! Damned opinionated drama freaks, damn you all! I'd wind chains around your necks if I could get my hands on you. I'd grind you into flour and shove you in the ovens! Oh, God, I can't get a grip on myself. When a man is being punished, he loses all sense of reason. I've got to pull myself together. But what first put it in my brain that he could be the inspector? Nothing. Suddenly everybody was talking about the inspector, the inspector. Who in hell first said he was the inspector? Answer me! It was Dobchinsky. No Bobchinsky. They came running in from the hotel like lunatics, screaming, "He's here, he's here!" He's here.

Z enters as an Officer in uniform.

Z   The government inspector from St. Petersburg has arrived with instructions from the Tsar. He demands your immediate attendance at the hotel.

THE END

www.ingramcontent.com/pod-product-compliance
Lightning Source LLC
Chambersburg PA
CBHW040417100526
44588CB00022B/2856